सीतारायाम्

rama jayam - likhita japam mala
-
simple (IV)

A Rama-Nama Journal
(Size 8.5"x8.5" Dotted Lines)
for
Writing the 'Rama' Name

राम जयम - लिखित जपम

राम-नाम माला सरल

राम-नाम लेखन पुस्तिका

Belongs to _____

Published by: **Rama-Nama Journals**
(an Imprint of e1i1 Corporation)

Title: **Rama Jayam - Likhita Japam Mala - Simple (IV)**
Sub-Title: **A Rama-Nama Journal (Size 8.5"x8.5" Dotted Lines) for Writing the 'Rama' Name**

Author: **Sushma**

Copyright Notice: **Copyright © e1i1 Corporation © Sushma**
All rights reserved. No part of this publication may be reproduced, distributed, or transmitted in any form or by any means, including photocopying, recording, or other electronic or mechanical methods.

Identifiers
ISBN: **978-1-945739-87-3** (Paperback)

—o—
www.**e1i1**.com -- www.**OnlyRama**.com
email: **e1i1**books**e1i1**@gmail.com

Our books can be bought online, or any bookstore. If a book is not available at your neighborhood bookstore they will be happy to order it for you. (Certain Hardcover Editions may not be immediately available—we apologize)

Some of our Current/Forthcoming Books are listed below. Please note that this is a partial list and that we are continually adding new books. Please visit www.**e1i1**.com / www.**onlyRama**.com for current offerings.

- **Tulsi Ramayana—The Hindu Bible:** Ramcharitmanas with English Translation & Transliteration
- **Ramcharitmanas:** Ramayana of Tulsidas with Transliteration (in English)
- **Ramayana, Large**: Tulsi Ramcharitmanas, Hindi only Edition, Large Font and Paper size
- **Ramayana, Medium**: Tulsi Ramcharitmanas, Hindi only Edition, Medium Font and Paper size
- **Ramayana, Small**: Tulsi Ramcharitmanas, Hindi only Edition, Small Font and Paper size
- **Sundarakanda:** The Fifth-Ascent of Tulsi Ramayana
- **RAMA GOD:** In the Beginning - Upanishad Vidya (Know Thyself)
- **Purling Shadows:** And A Dream Called Life - Upanishad Vidya (Know Thyself)
- **Fiery Circle:** Upanishad Vidya (Know Thyself)
- **Rama Hymns:** Hanuman-Chalisa, Rāma-Raksha-Stotra, Bhushundi-Ramayana, Nama-Ramayanam, Rāma-Shata-Nama-Stotra, etc. with Transliteration & English Translation
- **Rama Jayam - Likhita Japam :: Rama-Nama Mala** (several): Rama-Nama Journals for Writing the 'Rama' Name 100,000 Times
- **Tulsi-Ramayana Rama-Nama Mala** (multiple volumes): Legacy Journals for Writing the Rama Name alongside Tulsi Ramayana
- **Legacy Books - Endowment of Devotion** (multiple volumes): Legacy Journals for Writing the Rama Name alongside Sacred Hindu Texts

-- On our website may be found links to renditions of Rama Hymns –

rāma-nāma mahimā

In this modern era—which is awash with the six *Gunas* of *Māyā*: *Kāma* (Lust), *Krodha* (Anger), *Lobha* (Greed), *Moha* (Infatuation), *Mada* (Pride) & *Mātsarya* (Envy)—we find our minds sinking in worldliness. It seems that despite their best intent, no one can remain unsullied from the taints of Kali; this appears to be the fait-accompli of the *Kali-Yuga*—a very sad fate indeed. But despair not, because there is hope—we find ourselves assured.

The Japa of Rāma-Nāma (Rāma-Name) is the supreme path to salvation in this *Kali-Yuga*, assure our Scriptures; there is no Dharma higher than Nāma-Dharma in this Age of Kali—we are told. Sing the praises of the Lord and remain engaged in *Nāma-Smarana*—is the advice given to us by our saints. The chanting of Rāma-Nāma is The-One-Supreme-Path to escape the clutches of *Kali-Yuga*—declares Rāmacharitmānas—and in fact it is the one and only Dharma which is easy and feasible in the present times.

Many of the Hindu saints zealously assert: "In this Kali-Yuga, there is no other means, no other means, no other means of salvation—other than chanting the holy name Rāma, chanting the holy name Rāma, chanting the holy name Rāma."

Rāma-Japa—the constant repetition of the Supreme-Mantra 'Rāma'—is usually done mentally, or on a rosary; but there is one extremely efficacious method of this Japa: the *Likhita-Japa*, or the Written-Chant.

The practice of writing the Rāma Mantra over and over on paper is called the *Likhita-Japa*. This written form of Japa is a lasting record of your chant, remaining ever imbued with those holy vibrations, for all times, for the benefit of you and the future generations.

In India, as you may know, devotees of God have been chanting the name 'Rāma' and writing the Name 'Rāma'—pages upon pages of it, running into billions and billions, for ages. Hindu children are taught to write the Rāma-Nāma from their very childhood, and the writing competitions of the One *Lakh* Rāma–Nāma, brings up nostalgic memories for many Hindus.

The completed Rāma-Nāma books are variously utilized. Some devotees preserve them carefully for their holy association and divine energy, while others donate them to temples. The written Rāma-Nāma Books are used in the foundations of temples during construction; they add divine energy to the Temples—while in turn strengthening the foundations of the spiritual life of those who wrote the Rāma Name. Also some collected Rāma-Nāma books are placed in crypts to be used during *Yagna's* in Rāma Temples; and temples preserve these books for future. Devotees also place their own written Rāma-Nāma Books during the laying of foundation of their new homes, or in their *Pooja*-Room.

Of those of our Chakras (psychic centers), where our *Sanchit* (accumulated) Karmas are stored, Rāma is the *Beej Mantra*. The writing of Rāma-Nāma helps cleanse the Chakras, and our suppressed emotions, and the negative *Sanskaras* of the subconscious, and our remnant/unworked Karmas from past lives—which all get purged through the repetition of the Rāma-Nāma Mantra.

The chanting of Rāma-Nāma is a direct way to liberation. As per belief, devotees attempt to write down at least Eighty-Four Lakh (84,00,000) Rāma-Nāmas to get out of the birth-death cycle of Eighty-Four Lakh *Yonīs*, and thereby attain to salvation.

The *Likhita* Rāma-Nāma Japa is a powerful and transformative tool. As you write the Rāma-Nāma, all the senses become engaged in the service of Lord-God, and you find yourself simultaneously chanting and hearing and contemplating on the Lord—everything comes together naturally. This method clears away your thoughts and helps concentrate the entirety of your soul upon the Divine.

Any Japa is beneficial but somehow writing the Rāma-Nāma on paper brings up a great singularity of focus within the mind—and the peace of heart which ensues is something which is not so easily achieved with other forms of Japa. The written form of Rāma-Japa is somehow able to engage those parts of our body-mind continuum which other methods can not—and our meditative stance is able to achieve much deeper levels.

There is something special which will happen when you write the Rāma-Nāma—as you will discover. Peace and tranquility will surround you as you write the Supreme-Mantra: Rāma. The Rāma-Nāma will impart to you supreme strength, and great tolerance to withstand the vicissitudes of life. Bright unclouded wisdom will illumine your mind. You will find yourself in complete sense of surrender to your inner being. The resonance of God will resonate throughout your mind-body continuity. You will feel a flux of divine energy resonating within you. You will get great power and peace in your everyday life. The chanting of Rāma Mantra will protect your inner world as well as the outside.

Although the Rāma-Mantra is the gateway to higher consciousness and spiritual upliftment, but even at such junctures—when you find yourself in odd situations, where all the paths seem blocked—then just walking away from everything and simply writing the Rāma Nāma, will give you much needed clarity of thought—and a divine inspiration that will show the way out.

Thus, the Rāma Nāma is very transformative: with it you gain a balanced progress in your outside world and the inner. *Sant* Tulsidās says in *Rāmacharitmānas*: Place the Rāma-Nāma Jewel at the threshold, and there will be light both inside and out; i.e. a constant chant of the Rāma-Nāma from the mouth—the doorway to the body—will bring you external materialistic wellbeing, and also an inner spiritual wellness—both. Incredibly, with the Rāma-Nāma, you get to have the best of both the worlds.

According to the Vedas, just as the sun dispels the darkness, the chanting of Rāma-Nāma dispels all the evils and obstacles of life. The Rāma Nāma cures agony and showers the blessings of God; all righteous wishes get fulfilled; jealousy and pride disappear; life becomes imbued with satisfaction and peace; all of life's needs fall in place automatically—just like a miracle of nature guiding nature's forces. You may not always get what you want in the exact same form, but the Rāma-Nāma will purify things and bring to you the same needed happiness and bliss in a much more refined and lasting way. Your life will truly become filled with tranquility. Thus, with the Rāma-Nāma, an immense sense of spiritual wellbeing is experienced apart from gain of material happiness.

For *Likhita* Japa, you can write the Rāma-Nāma in any language of your choice—after all, Name is the connecting chord between the Divine and your inner self—but writing the Rāma-Nāma in its original Sanskrit form is simply superlative—most excellent, most effective. Sanskrit is *Deva-Bhāshā* (the language-of-gods). If you do not know how to write राम in Sanskrit it is quite easy. In the figure below, trace the contours 1-2 (which is the sound of underlined letters in the word '<u>r</u><u>u</u>n'), 3-4 (the sound of underlined letter <u>a</u> in '<u>a</u>rk'), 5-6 & 7-8 (the underlined <u>mu</u> in '<u>mu</u>st') and lastly the line 9-10; and that's it. Note the similarity of English **R**, **M** to the Sanskrit र, म, (and English words used here like *Name, Saint*—similar to the Sanskrit *Nāma, Sant*.) All European languages have their roots in Sanskrit, the great grand mother tongue of most.

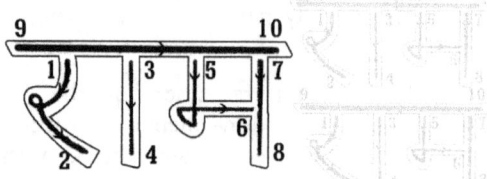

Write the Supreme-Mantra Rāma with reverence, every day, preferably at a set time, or as and when possible, in small measures, or copiously—howsoever your situation permits. There are no hard rules, do what feels good to your Soul. The important thing is to engage in the *Likhita-Japa*. When completed, you could keep the books in your Worship-Room, preserve them as treasures to pass on to future generations, donate them to Rāma Temples, or gift them to your loved ones—who will thereby inculcate crucial values from you, and learn the importance of the Rāma-Nāma, and get inspired with Hindu Values, especially so the younger ones.

While writing, focus your mind on the Rāma-Name and chant it within. Imagine Sītā-Rāma showering you with their bliss. Try to stay free of distractions, and with time you will find your mind taking a natural meditative stance when engaged in the written Rāma-Nāma Japa.

Traditionally people will write the Rāma Name in red ink on straight lines; but some devotees will also simultaneously make interesting designs—by changing the orientation of lines, or using different colors, or utilizing an underlying outline to base their Japa upon—the dotted grid should help with that. Also the dotted grid should allow you to write both ways—book oriented this way or rotated 90°—in case that's more convenient.

Find a set of pencils or pens which write and feel beautiful to you. If making an intricate pattern use pens that have finer points—but see that the ink does not bleed through to the other side.

Ideally, you will have a special set of pens kept purely for the Likhita Japa. This will make it easier for you to enter into the spirit of things. You will find that such implements—which you habitually use for holy tasks—build up energy and holy resonance.

You can choose any blank notebook or paper to write on, not necessarily this Journal. We wish you a Blissful Rāma-Nāma Japam.

※※※※※※※※※※※※※※※※※※※※※※※※

mātā rāmo mat-pitā rāma-candraḥ, svāmī rāmo mat-sakhā rāma-candraḥ, sarva-svaṁ me rāma-candro dayālu, rnā-nyaṁ jāne naiva jāne na jāne .

माता रामो मत्पिता रामचन्द्रः । स्वामी रामो मत्सखा रामचन्द्रः ॥ सर्वस्वं मे रामचन्द्रो दयालुः । नान्यं जाने नैव जाने न जाने ॥

राम राम

Rāma is my loving mother, and Rāma my protective father. Rāma is my gracious Lord, and Rāma my beloved friend. My everyone and everything is only Rāmachandra, the most-compassionate Lord. Other than Rāma I know of no other—absolutely, I know of no one except Shrī Rāma.

माता रामो मत्पिता रामचन्द्रः । स्वामी रामो मत्सखा रामचन्द्रः ॥ सर्वस्वं मे रामचन्द्रो दयालुः । नान्यं जाने नैव जाने न जाने ॥

mātā rāmo mat-pitā rāma-candraḥ, svāmī rāmo mat-sakhā rāma-candraḥ, sarva-svaṁ me rāma-candro dayālu, rnā-nyaṁ jāne naiva jāne na jāne

Rāma is my loving mother, and Rāma my protective father. Rāma is my gracious Lord, and Rāma my beloved friend. My everyone and everything is only Rāmachandra, the most-compassionate Lord. Other than Rāma I know of no other—absolutely, I know of no one except Shrī Rāma.

माता रामो मत्पिता रामचन्द्रः । स्वामी रामो मत्सखा रामचन्द्रः ॥ सर्वस्वं मे रामचन्द्रो दयालु । नान्यं जाने नैव जाने न जाने ॥

mātā rāmo mat-pitā rāma-candraḥ, svāmī rāmo mat-sakhā rāma-candraḥ, sarva-svaṁ me rāma-candro dayālu, rnā-nyaṁ jāne naiva jāne na jāne.

Rāma is my loving mother, and Rāma my protective father. Rāma is my gracious Lord, and Rāma my beloved friend. My everyone and everything is only Rāmachandra, the most-compassionate Lord. Other than Rāma I know of no other—absolutely, I know of no one except Shrī Rāma.

mātā rāmo mat-pitā rāma-candraḥ, svāmī rāmo mat-sakhā rāma-candraḥ, sarva-svaṁ me rāma-candro dayāluḥ, nānyaṁ jāne naiva jāne na jāne ।

माता रामो मत्पिता रामचन्द्रः । स्वामी रामो मत्सखा रामचन्द्रः ॥ सर्वस्वं मे रामचन्द्रो दयालुः । नान्यं जाने नैव जाने न जाने ॥

राम राम

Rāma is my loving mother, and Rāma my protective father. Rāma is my gracious Lord, and Rāma my beloved friend. My everyone and everything is only Rāmachandra, the most-compassionate Lord. Other than Rāma I know of no other,—absolutely, I know of no one except Shrī Rāma.

mātā rāmo mat-pitā rāma-candraḥ, svāmī rāmo mat-sakhā rāma-candraḥ, sarva-svaṁ me rāma-candro dayālu, rnā-nyaṁ naiva jāne na jāne

माता रामो मत्पिता रामचन्द्रः । स्वामी रामो मत्सखा रामचन्द्रः ॥ सर्वस्वं मे रामचन्द्रो दयालुः । नान्यं जाने नैव जाने न जाने ॥

Rāma is my loving mother, and Rāma my protective father. Rāma is my gracious Lord, and Rāma my beloved friend. My everyone and everything is only Rāmachandra, the most-compassionate Lord. Other than Rāma I know of no other—absolutely, I know of no one except Shrī Rāma.

mātā rāmo mat-pitā rāma-candraḥ, svāmī rāmo mat-sakhā rāma-candraḥ, sarva-svaṁ me rāma-candro dayāluḥ, nānyaṁ jāne naiva jāne na jāne ॥

माता रामो मत्पिता रामचन्द्रः । स्वामी रामो मत्सखा रामचन्द्रः ॥ सर्वस्वं मे रामचन्द्रो दयालुः । नान्यं जाने नैव जाने न जाने ॥

Rāma is my loving mother, and Rāma my protective father. Rāma is my gracious Lord, and Rāma my beloved friend. My everyone and everything is only Rāmachandra, the most-compassionate Lord. Other than Rāma I know of no other—absolutely, I know of no one except Shrī Rāma.

मata rāmo mat-pitā rāma-candraḥ , svāmī rāmo mat-sakhā rāma-candraḥ . sarva-svaṁ me rāma-candro dayālu , rnā-nyaṁ jāne naiva jāne na jāne .

माता रामो मत्पिता रामचन्द्रः । स्वामी रामो मत्सखा रामचन्द्रः ॥ सर्वस्वं मे रामचन्द्रो दयालुः । नान्यं जाने नैव जाने न जाने ॥

Rāma is my loving mother, and Rāma my protective father. Rāma is my gracious Lord, and Rāma my beloved friend. My everyone and everything is only Rāmachandra, the most-compassionate Lord. Other than Rāma I know of no other—absolutely, I know of no one except Shrī Rāma.

mātā rāmo mat-pitā rāma-candraḥ, svāmī rāmo mat-sakhā rāma-candraḥ. sarva-svaṁ me rāma-candro dayāluḥ, nānyaṁ jāne naiva jāne na jāne

माता रामो मत्पिता रामचन्द्रः। स्वामी रामो मत्सखा रामचन्द्रः॥ सर्वस्वं मे रामचन्द्रो दयालुः। नान्यं जाने नैव जाने न जाने॥

Rāma is my loving mother, and Rāma my protective father. Rāma is my gracious Lord, and Rāma my beloved friend. My everyone and everything is only Rāmachandra, the most-compassionate Lord. Other than Rāma I know of no other—absolutely, I know of no one except Shrī Rāma.

माता रामो मत्पिता रामचन्द्रः । स्वामी रामो मत्सखा रामचन्द्रः ॥ सर्वस्वं मे रामचन्द्रो दयालुः । नान्यं जाने नैव जाने न जाने ॥

mātā rāmo mat-pitā rāma-candraḥ, svāmī rāmo mat-sakhā rāma-candraḥ, sarva-svaṁ me rāma-candro dayālu, rnā-nyaṁ jāne naiva jāne na jāne

Rāma is my loving mother, and Rāma my protective father. Rāma is my gracious Lord, and Rāma my beloved friend. My everyone and everything is only Rāmachandra, the most-compassionate Lord. Other than Rāma I know of no other—absolutely, I know of no one except Shrī Rāma.

mātā rāmo mat-pitā rāma-candraḥ , svāmī rāmo mat-sakhā rāma-candraḥ . sarva-svaṁ me rāma-candro dayāluḥ , rnā-nyaṁ jāne naiva jāne na jāne

माता रामो मत्पिता रामचन्द्रः । स्वामी रामो मत्सखा रामचन्द्रः ॥ सर्वस्वं मे रामचन्द्रो दयालुः । नान्यं जाने नैव जाने न जाने ॥

Rāma is my loving mother, and Rāma my protective father. Rāma is my gracious Lord, and Rāma my beloved friend. My everyone and everything is only Rāmachandra, the most-compassionate Lord. Other than Rāma I know of no other—absolutely, I know of no one except Shrī Rāma.

mātā rāmo mat-pitā rāma-candraḥ, svāmī rāmo mat-sakhā rāma-candraḥ, sarva-svaṁ me rāma-candro dayāluḥ, rṇā-nyaṁ jāne naiva jāne na jāne ।

माता रामो मत्पिता रामचन्द्रः । स्वामी रामो मत्सखा रामचन्द्रः ॥ सर्वस्वं मे रामचन्द्रो दयालुः । नान्यं जाने नैव जाने न जाने ॥

राम राम

Rāma is my loving mother, and Rāma my protective father. Rāma is my gracious Lord, and Rāma my beloved friend. My everyone and everything is only Rāmachandra, the most compassionate Lord. Other than Rāma I know of no other—absolutely, I know of no one except Shrī Rāma.

माता रामो मत्पिता रामचन्द्रः । स्वामी रामो मत्सखा रामचन्द्रः ॥ सर्वस्वं मे रामचन्द्रो दयालुः । नान्यं जाने नैव जाने न जाने ॥

mātā rāmo mat-pitā rāma-candraḥ, svāmī rāmo mat-sakhā rāma-candraḥ, sarva-svaṁ me rāma-candro dayālu, rnā-nyaṁ jāne naiva jāne na jāne

Rāma is my loving mother, and Rāma my protective father. Rāma is my gracious Lord, and Rāma my beloved friend. My everyone and everything is only Rāmachandra, the most-compassionate Lord. Other than Rāma I know of no other—absolutely, I know of no one except Shrī Rāma.

माता रामो मत्पिता रामचन्द्रः । स्वामी रामो मत्सखा रामचन्द्रः ॥ सर्वस्वं मे रामचन्द्रो दयालुः । नान्यं जाने नैव जाने न जाने ॥

mātā rāmo mat-pitā rāma-candraḥ, svāmī rāmo mat-sakhā rāma-candraḥ, sarva-svaṁ me rāma-candro dayāluḥ, rnā-nyaṁ jāne naiva jāne na jāne

Rāma is my loving mother, and Rāma my protective father. Rāma is my gracious Lord, and Rāma my beloved friend. My everyone and everything is only Rāmachandra, the most compassionate Lord. Other than Rāma I know of no other—absolutely, I know of no one except Shrī Rāma.

माता रामो मत्पिता रामचन्द्रः । स्वामी रामो मत्सखा रामचन्द्रः । सर्वस्वं मे रामचन्द्रो दयालु नान्यं जाने नैव जाने न जाने ॥

mātā rāmo mat-pitā rāma-candraḥ, svāmī rāmo mat-sakhā rāma-candraḥ, sarva-svaṁ me rāma-candro dayālu, rnā-nyaṁ jāne naiva jāne na jāne ॥

Rāma is my loving mother, and Rāma my protective father. Rāma is my gracious Lord, and Rāma my beloved friend. My everyone and everything is only Rāmachandra, the most-compassionate Lord. Other than Rāma I know of no other—absolutely, I know of no one except Shrī Rāma.

māta rāmo mat-pitā rāma-candraḥ, svāmī rāmo mat-sakhā rāma-candraḥ, sarva-svaṁ me rāma-cando dayālu, nānyaṁ jāne naiva jāne na jāne．

माता रामो मत्पिता रामचन्द्रः । स्वामी रामो मत्सखा रामचन्द्रः ॥ सर्वस्वं मे रामचन्द्रो दयालुः । नान्यं जाने नैव जाने न जाने ॥

Rāma is my loving mother, and Rāma my protective father. Rāma is my gracious Lord, and Rāma my beloved friend. My everyone and everything is only Rāmachandra, the most-compassionate Lord. Other than Rāma I know of no other—absolutely, I know of no one except Shrī Rāma.

माता रामो मत्पिता रामचन्द्रः । स्वामी रामो मत्सखा रामचन्द्रः ॥ सर्वस्वं मे रामचन्द्रो दयालुः । नान्यं जाने नैव जाने न जाने ॥

mātā rāmo mat-pitā rāma-candraḥ, svāmī rāmo mat-sakhā rāma-candraḥ, sarva-svaṁ me rāma-candro dayālu, rnā-nyaṁ jāne naiva jāne na jāne

Rāma is my loving mother, and Rāma my protective father. Rāma is my gracious Lord, and Rāma my beloved friend. My everyone and everything is only Rāmachandra, the most-compassionate Lord. Other than Rāma I know of no other—absolutely, I know of no one except Shrī Rāma.

माता रामो मत्पिता रामचन्द्रः । स्वामी रामो मत्सखा रामचन्द्रः ॥ सर्वस्वं मे रामचन्द्रो दयालुः । नान्यं जाने नैव जाने न जाने ॥

mātā rāmo mat-pitā rāma-candraḥ, svāmī rāmo mat-sakhā rāma-candraḥ, sarva-svaṁ me rāma-candro dayāluḥ, rnā-nyaṁ jāne naiva jāne na jāne

Rāma is my loving mother, and Rāma my protective father. Rāma is my gracious Lord, and Rāma my beloved friend. My everyone and everything is only Rāmachandra, the most-compassionate Lord. Other than Rāma I know of no other—absolutely, I know of no one except Shrī Rāma.

mātā rāmo mat-pitā rāma-candraḥ , svāmī rāmo mat-sakhā rāma-candraḥ . sarva-svaṁ me rāma-candro dayālu , nānyaṁ jāne naiva jāne na jāne

माता रामो मत्पिता रामचन्द्रः । स्वामी रामो मत्सखा रामचन्द्रः ॥ सर्वस्वं मे रामचन्द्रो दयालु । नान्यं जाने नैव जाने न जाने ॥

Rāma is my loving mother, and Rāma my protective father. Rāma is my gracious Lord, and Rāma my beloved friend. My everyone and everything is only Rāmachandra, the most-compassionate Lord. Other than Rāma I know of no other—absolutely, I know of no one except Shrī Rāma.

माता रामो मत्-पिता रामचन्द्रः । स्वामी रामो मत्सखा रामचन्द्रः ॥
सर्वस्वं मे रामचन्द्रो दयालुः । नान्यं जाने नैव जाने न जाने ॥

mātā rāmo mat-pitā rāma-candraḥ, svāmī rāmo mat-sakhā rāma-candraḥ, sarva-svaṁ me rāma-candro dayālu, rnā-nyaṁ jāne naiva jāne na jāne ।

Rāma is my loving mother, and Rāma my protective father. Rāma is my gracious Lord, and Rāma my beloved friend. My everyone and everything is only Rāmachandra, the most-compassionate Lord. Other than Rāma I know of no other—absolutely, I know of no one except Shrī Rāma.

mātā rāmo mat-pitā rāmo rāma-candraḥ, svāmī rāmo mat-sakhā rāma-candraḥ, sarva-svaṁ me rāma-candro dayāluḥ, nānyaṁ jāne naiva jāne na jāne ।

माता रामो मत्पिता रामचन्द्रः । स्वामी रामो मत्सखा रामचन्द्रः ॥ सर्वस्वं मे रामचन्द्रो दयालुः । नान्यं जाने नैव जाने न जाने ॥

Rāma is my loving mother, and Rāma my protective father. Rāma is my gracious Lord, and Rāma my beloved friend. My everyone and everything is only Rāmachandra, the most compassionate Lord. Other than Rāma I know of no other—absolutely, I know of no one except Shrī Rāma.

mātā rāmo mat-pitā rāma-candraḥ, svāmī rāmo mat-sakhā rāma-candraḥ, sarva-svaṁ me rāma-candro dayāluḥ, ṛnā-nyaṁ jāne naiva jāne na jāne ।

माता रामो मत्पिता रामचन्द्रः । स्वामी रामो मत्सखा रामचन्द्रः ॥ सर्वस्वं मे रामचन्द्रो दयालु । नान्यं जाने नैव जाने न जाने ॥

Rāma is my loving mother, and Rāma my protective father. Rāma is my gracious Lord, and Rāma my beloved friend. My everyone and everything is only Rāmachandra, the most-compassionate Lord. Other than Rāma I know of no other—absolutely, I know of no one except Shrī Rāma.

mātā rāmo mat-pitā rāma-candraḥ , svāmī rāmo mat-sakhā rāma-candraḥ , sarva-svaṁ me rāma-candro dayālu , rnā-nyaṁ jāne naiva jāne na jāne ।

माता रामो मत्पिता रामचन्द्रः । स्वामी रामो मत्सखा रामचन्द्रः ॥ सर्वस्वं मे रामचन्द्रो दयालुः । नान्यं जाने नैव जाने न जाने ॥

राम राम

Rāma is my loving mother, and Rāma my protective father. Rāma is my gracious Lord, and Rāma my beloved friend. My everyone and everything is only Rāmachandra, the most-compassionate Lord. Other than Rāma I know of no other—absolutely, I know of no one except Shrī Rāma.

mātā rāmo mat-pitā rāma-candraḥ, svāmī rāmo mat-sakhā rāma-candraḥ, sarva-svaṁ me rāma-candro dayālu, rṇā-nyaṁ jāne naiva jāne na jāne ।

माता रामो मत्पिता रामचन्द्रः । स्वामी रामो मत्सखा रामचन्द्रः ॥ सर्वस्वं मे रामचन्द्रो दयालु । नान्यं जाने नैव जाने न जाने ॥

Rāma is my loving mother, and Rāma my protective father. Rāma is my gracious Lord, and Rāma my beloved friend. My everyone and everything is only Rāmachandra, the most-compassionate Lord. Other than Rāma I know of no other—absolutely, I know of no one except Shrī Rāma.

mātā rāmo mat-pitā rāmo rāma-candraḥ, svāmī rāmo mat-sakhā rāma-candraḥ, sarva-svaṁ me rāma-candro dayālu, rnā-nyaṁ jāne naiva jāne na jāne

माता रामो मत्पिता रामचन्द्रः । स्वामी रामो मत्सखा रामचन्द्रः ॥ सर्वस्वं मे रामचन्द्रो दयालु । नान्यं जाने नैव जाने न जाने ॥

Rāma is my loving mother, and Rāma my protective father. Rāma is my gracious Lord, and Rāma my beloved friend. My everyone and everything is only Rāmachandra, the most-compassionate Lord. Other than Rāma I know of no other—absolutely, I know of no one except Shrī Rāma.

माता रामो मत्पिता रामचन्द्रः । स्वामी रामो मत्सखा रामचन्द्रः । सर्वस्वं मे रामचन्द्रो दयालुः । नान्यं जाने नैव जाने न जाने ॥

mātā rāmo mat-pitā rāma-candraḥ, svāmī rāmo mat-sakhā rāma-candraḥ, sarva-svaṁ me rāma-candro dayālu, rnā-nyaṁ jāne naiva jāne na jāne

Rāma is my loving mother, and Rāma my protective father. Rāma is my gracious Lord, and Rāma my beloved friend. My everyone and everything is only Rāmachandra, the most-compassionate Lord. Other than Rāma I know of no other—absolutely, I know of no one except Shri Rāma.

mātā rāmo mat-pitā rāma-candraḥ , svāmī rāmo mat-sakhā rāma-candraḥ , sarva-svaṁ me rāma-candro dayāluḥ , rnā-nyaṁ jāne naiva jāne na jāne .

माता रामो मत्पिता रामचन्द्रः । स्वामी रामो मत्सखा रामचन्द्रः ॥ सर्वस्वं मे रामचन्द्रो दयालुः । नान्यं जाने नैव जाने न जाने ॥

Rāma is my loving mother, and Rāma my protective father. Rāma is my gracious Lord, and Rāma my beloved friend. My everyone and everything is only Rāmachandra, the most-compassionate Lord. Other than Rāma I know of no other—absolutely, I know of no one except Shrī Rāma.

mātā rāmo mat-pitā rāma-candraḥ, svāmī rāmo mat-sakhā rāma-candraḥ, sarva-svaṁ me rāma-candro dayāluḥ, nānyaṁ jāne naiva jāne na jāne ।

माता रामो मत्पिता रामचन्द्रः । स्वामी रामो मत्सखा रामचन्द्रः ॥ सर्वस्वं मे रामचन्द्रो दयालुः । नान्यं जाने नैव जाने न जाने ॥

Rāma is my loving mother, and Rāma my protective father. Rāma is my gracious Lord, and Rāma my beloved friend. My everyone and everything is only Rāmachandra, the most-compassionate Lord. Other than Rāma I know of no other—absolutely, I know of no one except Shrī Rāma.

mātā rāmo mat-pitā rāma-candraḥ, svāmī rāmo mat-sakhā rāma-candraḥ, sarva-svaṁ me rāma-candro dayālu, rnā-nyaṁ jāne naiva jāne na jāne．

माता रामो मत्पिता रामचन्द्रः। स्वामी रामो मत्सखा रामचन्द्रः॥ सर्वस्वं मे रामचन्द्रो दयालुः। नान्यं जाने नैव जाने न जाने॥

Rāma is my loving mother, and Rāma my protective father. Rāma is my gracious Lord, and Rāma my beloved friend. My everyone and everything is only Rāmachandra, the most-compassionate Lord. Other than Rāma I know of no other—absolutely, I know of no one except Shrī Rāma.

mātā rāmo mat-pitā rāma-candraḥ , svāmī rāmo mat-sakhā rāma-candraḥ ,
sarva-svaṁ me rāma-candro dayālu , rṅā-nyaṁ jāne naiva jāne na jāne ।

माता रामो मत्पिता रामचन्द्रः । स्वामी रामो मत्सखा रामचन्द्रः ॥ सर्वस्वं मे रामचन्द्रो दयालु । नान्यं जाने नैव जाने न जाने ॥

Rāma is my loving mother, and Rāma my protective father. Rāma is my gracious Lord, and Rāma my beloved friend. My everyone and everything is only Rāmachandra, the most-compassionate Lord. Other than Rāma I know of no other—absolutely, I know of no one except Shrī Rāma.

mātā rāmo mat-pitā rāma-candraḥ, svāmī rāmo mat-sakhā rāma-candraḥ. sarva-svaṁ me rāma-candro dayālu, rnā-nyaṁ jāne naiva jāne na jāne .

माता रामो मत्पिता रामचन्द्रः । स्वामी रामो मत्सखा रामचन्द्रः ॥ सर्वस्वं मे रामचन्द्रो दयालु । नान्यं जाने नैव जाने न जाने ॥

Rāma is my loving mother, and Rāma my protective father. Rāma is my gracious Lord, and Rāma my beloved friend. My everyone and everything is only Rāmachandra, the most-compassionate Lord. Other than Rāma I know of no other—absolutely, I know of no one except Shrī Rāma.

mātā rāmo mat-pitā rāma-candraḥ, svāmī rāmo mat-sakhā rāma-candraḥ, sarva-svaṁ me rāma-candro dayālu, rṇā-nyaṁ jāne naiva jāne na jāne.

माता रामो मत्पिता रामचन्द्रः । स्वामी रामो मत्सखा रामचन्द्रः ॥ सर्वस्वं मे रामचन्द्रो दयालु । नान्यं जाने नैव जाने न जाने ॥

Rāma is my loving mother, and Rāma my protective father. Rāma is my gracious Lord, and Rāma my beloved friend. My everyone and everything is only Rāmachandra, the most compassionate Lord. Other than Rāma I know of no other—absolutely, I know of no one except Shrī Rāma.

mātā rāmo mat-pitā rāma-candraḥ, svāmī rāmo rāma-candraḥ,
माता रामो मत्पिता रामचन्द्रः । स्वामी रामो

svāmī rāmo mat-sakhā rāma-candraḥ, sarva-svaṁ me rāma-candro dayālu,
स्वामी रामो मत्सखा रामचन्द्रः ॥ सर्वस्वं मे रामचन्द्रो दयालु

rāma-nyaṁ jāne naiva jāne na jāne .
रनान्यं जाने नैव जाने न जाने ॥

Rāma is my loving mother, and Rāma my protective father. Rāma is my gracious Lord, and Rāma my beloved friend. My everyone and everything is only Rāmachandra, the most compassionate Lord. Other than Rāma I know of no other—absolutely, I know of no one except Shrī Rāma.

माता रामो मत्पिता रामचन्द्रः । स्वामी रामो मत्सखा रामचन्द्रः ॥ सर्वस्वं मे रामचन्द्रो दयालुः । नान्यं जाने नैव जाने न जाने ॥

mātā rāmo mat-pitā rāma-candraḥ , svāmī rāmo mat-sakhā rāma-candraḥ , sarva-svaṁ me rāma-candro dayāluḥ , rnā-nyaṁ jāne naiva jāne na jāne .

Rāma is my loving mother, and Rāma my protective father. Rāma is my gracious Lord, and Rāma my beloved friend. My everyone and everything is only Rāmachandra, the most-compassionate Lord. Other than Rāma I know of no other—absolutely, I know of no one except Shri Rāma.

mātā rāmo mat-pitā rāmo mat-pitā rāma-candraḥ , svāmī rāmo mat-sakhā rāma-candraḥ . sarva-svaṁ me rāma-candro dayālu , rṇā-nyaṁ jāne naiva jāne na jāne .

माता रामो मत्पिता रामचन्द्रः । स्वामी रामो मत्सखा रामचन्द्रः ॥ सर्वस्वं मे रामचन्द्रो दयालु । नान्यं जाने नैव जाने न जाने ॥

Rāma is my loving mother, and Rāma my protective father. Rāma is my gracious Lord, and Rāma my beloved friend. My everyone and everything is only Rāmachandra, the most-compassionate Lord. Other than Rāma I know of no other—absolutely, I know of no one except Shrī Rāma.

माता रामो मत्पिता रामचन्द्रः । स्वामी रामो मत्सखा रामचन्द्रः । सर्वस्वं मे रामचन्द्रो दयालुः । नान्यं जाने नैव जाने न जाने ॥

mātā rāmo mat-pitā rāma-candraḥ, svāmī rāmo mat-sakhā rāma-candraḥ, sarva-svaṁ me rāma-candro dayāluḥ, rnā-nyaṁ jāne naiva jāne na jāne

Rāma is my loving mother, and Rāma my protective father. Rāma is my gracious Lord, and Rāma my beloved friend. My everyone and everything is only Rāmachandra, the most compassionate Lord. Other than Rāma I know of no other—absolutely, I know of no one except Shrī Rāma.

mātā rāmo mat-pitā rāma-candraḥ, svāmī rāmo mat-sakhā rāma-candraḥ, sarva-svaṁ me rāma-candro dayāluḥ, nā-nyaṁ jāne naiva jāne na jāne ।

माता रामो मत्पिता रामचन्द्रः । स्वामी रामो मत्सखा रामचन्द्रः ॥ सर्वस्वं मे रामचन्द्रो दयालुः । नान्यं जाने नैव जाने न जाने ॥

Rāma is my loving mother, and Rāma my protective father. Rāma is my gracious Lord, and Rāma my beloved friend. My everyone and everything is only Rāmachandra, the most compassionate Lord. Other than Rāma I know of no other—absolutely, I know of no one except Shrī Rāma.

माता रामो मत्-पिता रामचन्द्रः । स्वामी रामो मत्सखा रामचन्द्रः ॥
सर्वस्वं मे रामचन्द्रो दयालुः । नान्यं जाने नैव जाने न जाने ॥

mātā rāmo mat-pitā rāma-candraḥ, svāmī rāmo mat-sakhā rāma-candraḥ, sarva-svaṁ me rāma-candro dayāluḥ, rnā-nyaṁ jāne naiva jāne na jāne

Rāma is my loving mother, and Rāma my protective father. Rāma is my gracious Lord, and Rāma my beloved friend. My everyone and everything is only Rāmachandra, the most-compassionate Lord. Other than Rāma I know of no other—absolutely, I know of no one except Shrī Rāma.

mātā rāmo mat-pitā rāma-candraḥ, svāmī rāmo mat-sakhā rāma-candraḥ, sarva-svaṁ me rāma-candro dayāluḥ, rnā-nyaṁ jāne naiva jāne na jāne ।

माता रामो मत्पिता रामचन्द्रः । स्वामी रामो मत्सखा रामचन्द्रः ॥ सर्वस्वं मे रामचन्द्रो दयालुः । नान्यं जाने नैव जाने न जाने ॥

राम राम

Rāma is my loving mother, and Rāma my protective father. Rāma is my gracious Lord, and Rāma my beloved friend. My everyone and everything is only Rāmachandra, the most-compassionate Lord. Other than Rāma I know of no other—absolutely, I know of no one except Shrī Rāma.

mātā rāmo mat-pitā rāma-candraḥ, svāmī rāmo mat-sakhā rāma-candraḥ, sarva-svaṁ me rāma-candro dayālu, rnā-nyaṁ jāne naiva jāne na jāne.

माता रामो मत्पिता रामचन्द्रः । स्वामी रामो मत्सखा रामचन्द्रः ॥ सर्वस्वं मे रामचन्द्रो दयालु । नान्यं जाने नैव जाने न जाने ॥

Rāma is my loving mother, and Rāma my protective father. Rāma is my gracious Lord, and Rāma my beloved friend. My everyone and everything is only Rāmachandra, the most-compassionate Lord. Other than Rāma I know of no other—absolutely, I know of no one except Shrī Rāma.

mātā rāmo mat-pitā rāma-candraḥ, svāmī rāmo mat-sakhā rāma-candraḥ, sarva-svaṁ me rāma-candro dayālu, rṇā-nyaṁ jāne naiva jāne na jāne ।

माता रामो मत्पिता रामचन्द्रः । स्वामी रामो मत्सखा रामचन्द्रः ॥ सर्वस्वं मे रामचन्द्रो दयालुः । नान्यं जाने नैव जाने न जाने ॥

Rāma is my loving mother, and Rāma my protective father. Rāma is my gracious Lord, and Rāma my beloved friend. My everyone and everything is only Rāmachandra, the most-compassionate Lord. Other than Rāma I know of no other—absolutely, I know of no one except Shrī Rāma.

माता रामो मत्पिता रामचन्द्रः । स्वामी रामो मत्सखा रामचन्द्रः ॥ सर्वस्वं मे रामचन्द्रो दयालुः । नान्यं जाने नैव जाने न जाने ॥

mātā rāmo mat-pitā rāma-candraḥ, svāmī rāmo mat-sakhā rāma-candraḥ, sarva-svaṁ me rāma-candro dayāluḥ, rnā-nyaṁ jāne naiva jāne na jāne

Rāma is my loving mother, and Rāma my protective father. Rāma is my gracious Lord, and Rāma my beloved friend. My everyone and everything is only Rāmachandra, the most-compassionate Lord. Other than Rāma I know of no other—absolutely, I know of no one except Shrī Rāma.

mātā rāmo mat-pitā rāma-candraḥ, svāmī rāmo mat-sakhā rāma-candraḥ, sarva-svaṁ me rāma-candro dayālu, ṛnā-nyaṁ jāne naiva jāne na jāne.

माता रामो मत्पिता रामचन्द्रः । स्वामी रामो मत्सखा रामचन्द्रः ॥ सर्वस्वं मे रामचन्द्रो दयालुः । नान्यं जाने नैव जाने न जाने ॥

Rāma is my loving mother, and Rāma my protective father. Rāma is my gracious Lord, and Rāma my beloved friend. My everyone and everything is only Rāmachandra, the most-compassionate Lord. Other than Rāma I know of no other—absolutely, I know of no one except Shrī Rāma.

mātā rāmo mat-pitā rāma-candraḥ, svāmī rāmo mat-sakhā rāma-candraḥ, sarva-svaṁ me rāma-candro dayāluḥ, nānyaṁ jāne naiva jāne na jāne ।

माता रामो मत्पिता रामचन्द्रः । स्वामी रामो मत्सखा रामचन्द्रः ॥ सर्वस्वं मे रामचन्द्रो दयालुः । नान्यं जाने नैव जाने न जाने ॥

Rāma is my loving mother, and Rāma my protective father. Rāma is my gracious Lord, and Rāma my beloved friend. My everyone and everything is only Rāmachandra, the most-compassionate Lord. Other than Rāma I know of no other—absolutely, I know of no one except Shrī Rāma.

mātā rāmo mat-pitā rāma-candraḥ , svāmī rāmo mat-sakhā rāma-candraḥ , sarva-svaṁ me rāma-candro dayālu , rnā-nyaṁ jāne naiva jāne na jāne ।

माता रामो मत्पिता रामचन्द्रः । स्वामी रामो मत्सखा रामचन्द्रः ॥ सर्वस्वं मे रामचन्द्रो दयालुः । नान्यं जाने नैव जाने न जाने ॥

Rāma is my loving mother, and Rāma my protective father. Rāma is my gracious Lord, and Rāma my beloved friend. My everyone and everything is only Rāmachandra, the most-compassionate Lord. Other than Rāma I know of no other—absolutely, I know of no one except Shrī Rāma.

mātā rāmo mat-pitā rāma-candraḥ, svāmī rāmo mat-sakhā rāma-candraḥ, sarva-svaṁ me rāma-candro dayālu, rnā-nyaṁ jāne naiva jāne na jāne.

माता रामो मत्पिता रामचन्द्रः । स्वामी रामो मत्सखा रामचन्द्रः ॥ सर्वस्वं मे रामचन्द्रो दयालु । नान्यं जाने नैव जाने न जाने ॥

Rāma is my loving mother, and Rāma my protective father. Rāma is my gracious Lord, and Rāma my beloved friend. My everyone and everything is only Rāmachandra, the most-compassionate Lord. Other than Rāma I know of no other—absolutely, I know of no one except Shrī Rāma.

mātā rāmo mat-pitā rāma-candraḥ, svāmī rāmo mat-sakhā rāma-candraḥ, sarva-svaṁ me rāma-candro dayālu, rṇā-nyaṁ jāne naiva jāne na jāne ।
माता रामो मत्पिता रामचन्द्रः । स्वामी रामो मत्सखा रामचन्द्रः ॥ सर्वस्वं मे रामचन्द्रो दयालुः । नान्यं जाने नैव जाने न जाने ॥

Rāma is my loving mother, and Rāma my protective father. Rāma is my gracious Lord, and Rāma my beloved friend. My everyone and everything is only Rāmachandra, the most-compassionate Lord. Other than Rāma I know of no other—absolutely, I know of no one except Shrī Rāma.

माता रामो मत्-पिता राम-चन्द्रः, स्वामी रामो मत्-सखा राम-चन्द्रः ।
माता रामो मत्पिता रामचन्द्रः । स्वामी रामो मत्सखा रामचन्द्रः ॥

सर्व-स्वं मे राम-चन्द्रो दयालुः, र्ना-न्यं जाने नैव जाने न जाने ।
सर्वस्वं मे रामचन्द्रो दयालुः । नान्यं जाने नैव जाने न जाने ॥

Rāma is my loving mother, and Rāma my protective father. Rāma is my gracious Lord, and Rāma my beloved friend. My everyone and everything is only Rāmachandra, the most-compassionate Lord. Other than Rāma I know of no other—absolutely, I know of no one except Shrī Rāma.

माता रामो मत्पिता रामचन्द्रः । स्वामी रामो मत्सखा रामचन्द्रः ॥ सर्वस्वं मे रामचन्द्रो दयालु र्नान्यं जाने नैव जाने न जाने ॥

mātā rāmo mat-pitā rāma-candraḥ, svāmī rāmo mat-sakhā rāma-candraḥ . sarva-svaṁ me rāma-candro dayālu , rnā-nyaṁ jāne naiva jāne na jāne .

Rāma is my loving mother, and Rāma my protective father. Rāma is my gracious Lord, and Rāma my beloved friend. My everyone and everything is only Rāmachandra, the most-compassionate Lord. Other than Rāma I know of no other—absolutely, I know of no one except Shrī Rāma.

माता रामो मत्-पिता रामचन्द्रः । स्वामी रामो मत्सखा रामचन्द्रः ॥ सर्वस्वं मे रामचन्द्रो दयालु । नान्यं जाने नैव जाने न जाने ॥

mātā rāmo mat-pitā rāma-candraḥ, svāmī rāmo mat-sakhā rāma-candraḥ. sarva-svaṁ me rāma-candro dayālu, rnā-nyaṁ jāne naiva jāne na jāne .

Rāma is my loving mother, and Rāma my protective father. Rāma is my gracious Lord, and Rāma my beloved friend. My everyone and everything is only Rāmachandra, the most-compassionate Lord. Other than Rāma I know of no other—absolutely, I know of no one except Shrī Rāma.

mātā rāmo mat-pitā rāma-candraḥ, svāmī rāmo mat-sakhā rāma-candraḥ, sarva-svaṁ me rāma-candro dayālu, rnā-nyaṁ jāne naiva jāne na jāne

माता रामो मत्पिता रामचन्द्रः । स्वामी रामो मत्सखा रामचन्द्रः ॥ सर्वस्वं मे रामचन्द्रो दयालु । नान्यं जाने नैव जाने न जाने ॥

राम राम

Rāma is my loving mother, and Rāma my protective father. Rāma is my gracious Lord, and Rāma my beloved friend. My everyone and everything is only Rāmachandra, the most-compassionate Lord. Other than Rāma I know of no other—absolutely, I know of no one except Shrī Rāma.

मātā rāmo mat-pitā rāma-candraḥ, svāmī rāmo mat-sakhā rāma-candraḥ, sarva-svaṁ me rāma-candro dayālu, rṇā-nyaṁ jāne naiva jāne na jāne

माता रामो मत्पिता रामचन्द्रः । स्वामी रामो मत्सखा रामचन्द्रः ॥ सर्वस्वं मे रामचन्द्रो दयालु । नान्यं जाने नैव जाने न जाने ॥

Rāma is my loving mother, and Rāma my protective father. Rāma is my gracious Lord, and Rāma my beloved friend. My everyone and everything is only Rāmachandra, the most-compassionate Lord. Other than Rāma I know of no other—absolutely, I know of no one except Shrī Rāma.

mātā rāmo mat-pitā rāma-candraḥ, svāmī rāmo mat-sakhā rāma-candraḥ, sarva-svaṁ me rāma-candro dayālu, rṇā-nyaṁ jāne naiva jāne na jāne.

माता रामो मत्पिता रामचन्द्रः । स्वामी रामो मत्सखा रामचन्द्रः ॥ सर्वस्वं मे रामचन्द्रो दयालुः । नान्यं जाने नैव जाने न जाने ॥